Praise for Todd Davis

... it's time to recognize what an important voice in American poetry we have in Todd Davis.

—Image

As readers encounter the ordinary miracles that Davis reveals as both father and son within "the kingdom of the ditch," they also are reminded that the human is not apart from nature but a part of it.

—Chicago Tribune

These poems are really lyric meditations on the way life and the world turns, done in stillness yet shared through a poet's trust in the world and the word. ... We can only be grateful for this music of living, for such a song and such a singer.

—New York Journal of Books

The poems that comprise *In the Kingdom of the Ditch* hold quiet wisdom, not unlike the solemnity and silence of personal prayer.

—Los Angeles Review

Davis hunts, fishes, and observes nature in the great tradition of Robert Frost, James Dickey, and Jim Harrison, among others. His poems lead us from the tangible to the intangible and about halfway back again.

—Gray's Sporting Journal

The beauty of this work is that Davis takes the seed of impermanence in every living thing and shows it growing to the good. This is the transformative power of poetry. ... Davis does not need tactics or strategies. He has the dignity of the best word at his command, and there is in this book no space between great and good.

—Washington Independent Review of Books

Davis's poems focus on sacrament, prayer, and religion; each one is a meditation of thanks, urging the reader to love life. ... Wisdom, more than anything, characterizes his poems.

—& Letters

WINTERKILL

WINTERKILL

POEMS BY TODD DAVIS

MICHIGAN STATE UNIVERSITY PRESS ▪ *East Lansing*

 Michigan State University Press
East Lansing, Michigan 48823-5245

Printed and bound in the United States of America.

22 21 20 19 18 17 16   1 2 3 4 5 6 7 8 9 10

Library of Congress Control Number: 2015939573
ISBN: 978-1-61186-196-9 (pbk.)
ISBN: 978-1-60917-482-8 (ebook: PDF)
ISBN: 978-1-62895-257-5 (ebook: ePub)
ISBN: 978-1-62896-257-4 (ebook: Kindle)

Book design by Charlie Sharp, Sharp Des!gns, Lansing, Michigan
Cover design by Erin Kirk New
Cover artwork is *Fox Hunt*, 1893 Winslow Homer (38x68.5 inches, oil on
canvas, Acc. No. 1894.4) and is used courtesy of the Pennsylvania Academy
of the Fine Arts, Philadelphia. Joseph E. Temple Fund.

g green
press Michigan State University Press is a member of the Green Press
INITIATIVE Initiative and is committed to developing and encouraging
ecologically responsible publishing practices. For more information about
the Green Press Initiative and the use of recycled paper in book publishing,
please visit *www.greenpressinitiative.org*.

Visit Michigan State University Press at *www.msupress.org*

As always
For Shelly, Noah, & Nathan

There is another world, but it is in this one.

WILLIAM BUTLER YEATS

Contents

WINTERKILL

Nicrophorus

of the family Silphidae

Death-loving to the point

      of monogamy, we carry

the corpse of the world

      on our feet, shuffling forward

to a suitable burial, to the pit

      we've dug that consumes

what we love, and feeds

      those who come after us.

I.

Homily

O I say these are not the parts and poems of the Body only,
but of the Soul,
O I say now these are the Soul!
—WALT WHITMAN

By the second week in September nuthatches capture the last
elderberries, excrement purpled and extravagant, sprayed
drunkenly across my truck's hood. I've been thinking about the God
I pray to with no lasting effect and note the effortless work
the stream does as it feeds these bushes. My father was baptized
in the Green River, led by the hand in white robes to be dunked
beneath the current. Sometimes when mother gathers sheets
from the clothesline in late summer, she finds the droppings
of a bluebird written like a sacred text. But what saint could decipher it?
In a field reclaimed by clover, I sprawl sideways and count
the small green hands of the leaves enfolding me. The gentle *sshh,*
sshh of the wind dismisses my garbled words as they break
the water's surface or cross over the low hum of bees. Eventually
we have to ascend to breathe, accepting the uncertainty of the air
above our heads. At dusk a skein of geese skitters in a half-formed V,
and a skulk of fox pups gnaw at each other's throats in a game
to prepare for death. Salvation is supposed to be sweet, like the sugar
of a wild grape, but where would we be without the fossil record to lead?
All of us are worth saving, despite the stink we've made since learning
to walk upright 400,000 years ago. As a boy, when a calf got scours,
my father would search the field for lamb's ear, collecting its velvet
leaves to better dress the open sores that ran the length of the flanks.
His mother told him mercy is all Jesus wants of anyone. I believe,
despite my unbelief. When the Belgian drapes its sorrel neck
across the paddock gate, I offer him two handfuls of clover
I painstakingly picked.

Phenology: Actias luna

I've been afraid of your going, which was inevitable,
like the luna moth that wakes, makes love, lays

her eggs on the bottom sides of leaves, then dies.
Everything transpires. This moth that lives only a week,

born without a mouth. The painting you gave me that holds
a tree in the center, branches decorated with hands and feet,

each with lips saying their names. When I speak your name,
I feel the soft brush of insect wings across my cheek.

Afterlife

When the owl came down

      through the branches of an oak,

having left its perch in a black cherry

      where my son sat in a ladder-stand

waiting for deer to trail the old ravine,

      its face was illuminated by the last

of the moon, wings nearly silent,

      my dead father's face staring at me,

grinning with rings of feathers

      and a plump shrew dangling

from its beak.

Sulphur Hatch

Tonight our son is on the river
that runs through the upper pasture.
The cattle low as he loops
a nearly invisible line
into the air.

Above the water sulphurs hatch
and trout begin to surface.
The sun descends between
a water gap that joins Bell's Run
to our river.

The sky this time of night
whitens to the color of a blackberry
blossom, and a kingfisher flies
out of a sycamore to dive
at the spine of a trout.

Yesterday we found a fish,
gray and stiff, at the clear bottom
of the stream. We tossed it
onto the bank, hoping a raccoon
might scavenge it.

In this half-light, our boy is walking
home across the early June hay.
Each step he takes
leaves a shadowed space
we'll see come morning.

Mud Dauber

Work with a hammer teaches us: blood under the nail
forms a half-moon. A fist at the side of the head teaches us:

blood on the tongue tastes like sun-warmed iron.
Blood itches as it dries the jagged lines

the locust thorn leaves, while chamber by chamber
the nest grows on the underside of an old board.

Yesterday my youngest was stung by a wasp, foot swelling
twice its size. As we sit on the porch after dinner, barn swallows

fly in and out of the loft, bellies the color of sky at dusk.
Only in this new dark does the buzzing finally stop.

In a Dream William Stafford Visits Me

He is walking across a field of wheat
in Kansas, grain as tall as his shoulder
and as tan as his face. He is cupping his hands
to his mouth, shouting words the wind steals
and throws into the air like chaff. I need to know
what he's said and begin chasing his voice as it scuttles
across the ground like a sheaf of newsprint.
He, too, is running, but on a slender path in Oregon
cut by the hooves of ungulates. For someone
who's been dead nearly twenty years, he is remarkably fit,
and I can't catch him until he stops at the bottom of the hill
where a stream washes on toward a bay. He says
the sea knows mistakes he has made. He says
the tides have told the world about them.

He points to the sky, and my eye follows
into the tops of these finely needled trees
where darkness and light marry. He asks
for a glass of water, and I realize he is laid out
on our couch downstairs, head propped on a pillow,
left arm bending like a basket to cradle his thick
mat of hair. The lamp on the end table sheds a circle
of light, and he muses about what is hidden
between the pine cone's creased tongues. I stumble
over the Latin for lodgepole, *pinus contorta*,
and tell him this tree must have fire
to release its seed. He is writing on a legal pad
in his barely legible scrawl. I make out the words
let and *fire* and *come.*

By the Rivers of Babylon

The father of a boy my son plays basketball with
overdosed last week. Out of prison less than two days, he slid
the needle into that place where he wanted to feel something
like God and pushed the plunger of the syringe. The boy isn't any good
at sports, but when the coach subs him late in the game, score
already settled, we cheer wildly, as if he's performed a miracle,
when he makes a layup or snares a rebound. Heroin is sold
in narrow spaces between row houses in the first few blocks
that rise from the railroad tracks and train shops. This part of town
still looks like the 1950s, if the soft pastels of that decade
had crumbled to gravel and ash. The boy lives with his grandmother
in a curtained white house near the cathedral. His mother,
who lost custody when he was five, is back in jail for possession.
At the funeral, my son and his friends pat the boy on the shoulder,
mumble they're sorry after the mass, then usher him to the pizza shop
where they eat as many slices as their stomachs will hold.
In Pennsylvania, if you keep your eyes on the horizon,
the mountains look heavenly. The white lines that snake
through the gaps in winter become streams that hold
the most delicate fish. As the snowpack melts,
there's more water than we know what to do with,
all of it rushing toward the valley and the muddy river
whose banks keep washing away.

Drouth

That's what we called it, locked in the speech
our father spoke, like the farm pond we dug in '74,
war already having buried our brother

in the mud of another country. First a few days
without rain, then a string even longer,
until there was nothing for three months.

The melons in the far field shriveled like corpses,
and the water dropped from twelve feet to half that.
Soon the dark light farther down began to fade.

Fish lost the paths they followed in the weeds,
bodies floating to the top where we skimmed them
to scatter in the fields. We sowed scaled carcasses

where corn was supposed to be, hoping the smell
wouldn't choke us, hoping the wind wouldn't come
from the south. We'd been taught to waste nothing,

taught that fish, when caught and opened to rot,
can call down rain, swim into soil's cracks,
fins becoming stalks, reborn into green blades.

After the Third Concussion

As fewer and fewer leaves remain, the woods brighten

     like a minnow's flash in a stream that has shrunk

from July's heat. With more light the moss greens

     to the shade of a football field where a groundskeeper

spreads nitrogen and runs the sprinklers all night.

     In the left drawer of my desk, wrapped in paper towel,

sit three claws I salvaged from a bear's rotting foot.

     He died in January—first thaw,

then days of cold rain. What else can you do

     once hunger awakens you? Two nights ago

the moon's white and the river's black plaited themselves

     into silver braids, devouring my grandmother's hair.

As the sun rose like a peach, juice dripping

     on summer's chin, the spear of fish that skulks

the shallows slept, and the stars above my head

     went out, one by one.

What My Neighbor Tells Me
Isn't Global Warming

Two hours west in Pittsburgh my friend's snow peas blossom, only
mid-April and his lettuce already good for three weeks. Whenever my
neighbor and I meet at our mailboxes, he tells me, *Global warming's a
bunch of bullshit*, the same way you or I might say, *How's the weather?*
or, *Sure could use some rain*. It's a strange salutation, but he's convinced
the president is a communist. I keep asking my wife if any of this is
going to change. I think she's tired of my questions. Yesterday our
son wrote a letter to give to his girlfriend after he breaks up. He says
he's real sorry. So am I. The tears they'll cry are no different than our
cat's wailing to be let out, despite the rain that's been falling since
dawn. The three donkeys that graze in the pasture share the field
with exactly eleven horses. It's instructive that the horses don't lord it
over the donkeys that they're horses. For two straight weeks in March
it was thirty degrees warmer than it should've been. Last night the
moon shot up brighter than I've ever seen it, a giant eyeball staring us
down, or one of those lightbulbs that's supposed to last for five years.
The weatherman called it perigee on the six o'clock news, so I walked
to the pasture to see if it made any difference to the donkeys. Each
time a horse shuffled its hooves and spread its legs to piss or fart, the
shadow looked like a rocket lifting off. Awe and wonder is what I feel
after a quarter century of marriage. My wife just shakes her head when
I say her right ankle is like a wood lily's stem, as silky and delicate as
that flower's blossom. If she'd let me, I'd slide my hand over her leg
for hours without a trace of boredom. This past week largemouth bass
started spawning in the weeds close to shore, patrolling back and forth
with a singular focus. You can drag a popper or buzzbait right in front
of them and they'll ignore it. All this land we live on was stripped for
timber and coal a century ago. We still find lumps, hard and black,
beneath the skin. Now it's fracking for natural gas. Can you imagine?
We're actually breaking the plates on purpose. I know what my
grandmother would've said about that. Last time, before the mining

and timber companies pulled up stakes, they brought in dozers that raked what little soil was left, planted thin grasses and pine trees. With the real forest gone, warm wind funnels through the gaps in the ridges, turns the giant turbine blades we've bolted to the tops of mountains.

For Jim Daniels

Grievous

> *And these deer at my bramble gate: so close*
> *here, we touch our own kind in each other.*
> —TU FU

Near the railroad tracks poachers

    have stacked the bodies of seven

headless deer, stuffed sacks

    of flesh to waste. Someone has dumped

a horse head, too. I can't imagine

    why, or what was done with a body

of such heft. Hair stripped, the hum

    of bluebottle flies pervades the rotting

air. I note the lips are lost as well

    to bacteria and beetles that crave the flesh.

Large teeth protrude like a piano's

    keys, bringing back the song I sang

while planting the corn and squash

    I knew the deer would eat.

Yu

Blue dragonflies rise
from the alder marsh
in the last hour of light,
and barn swallows skim
the field to filch the heads
of the tallest grasses,
hungering for these blue
seraphs who open
into the stomach's
afterlife. Wings thin
as wafers carry us
into the resurrection
of dirt or limb
or wherever
plundered flight
may come to rest.
Dragonflies know
the closer to earth
the safer the path.
Swallows cannot dive
from heaven
without crashing
into catkins and cattails,
the blessed covering
of darkness
that drapes this world—
which is not made
of ten thousand things
but ten thousand
thousand.

Wu

In the woods where I remember nothing

      a boulder sits, and around its base

hay-scented fern dies the dun-colored yellow

      of its brief death. Above my head only silence,

then the sound of a Cooper's hawk

      followed by the absence of that sound.

After Reading Han Shan

A grouse flushes, flies over the stream, water flowing high
so I can't hear the bird's winged-drumming.

In the river the gate of an abandoned shopping cart swings
in the current, inviting fish to swim in its basket.

Hearing crows talk, I've come to accept their intelligence rivals ours.
They remember the architecture of human faces even longer.

Near the seep, where the stream starts, turkey tracks crisscross:
brush strokes of a poet who smiles at the clarity of mud.

The moon mewls above tamaracks, golden needles
raking the sky. Each year I wait for certain days to return.

As I walk this path, I remember Han Shan wrote poems on rocks
and trees, the parchment of cliffs. Some say he vanished

into a crevice in the mountain. In the ravine that divides
the mountains I live between, porcupine and bear disappear

behind rock outcroppings, and from the bluffs at day's end
coyotes scream their thanks.

Cenotaph

I dream my dead father
spends most
of the afternoon's hours
stacking rock he gathers
from the dried riverbed.

Drought means
he must carry
five-gallon buckets
to water the tomatoes
and kale, the wilting
Brussels sprouts.

Stone walls ring
my parents' acreage,
lines of demarcation
like those that tell
the age of a tree.

Winter heaves
rocks
to the ground,
and in spring
my father
lifts them back
to their rightful
place.

He calls them
monuments to dearth,
to lack's own beauty
and what it allows
him to make.

Crow's Murder

Crow felt something that wasn't her body lift
toward the topmost boughs of the white pine,

and in this awkward rising noticed the wings
she loved and sailed upon didn't beat anymore.

She could see her own body collapsed on the ground
in the same way she saw the image of her crow-self

flying over the lake when no wind moved the water.
A rivulet of blood formed beneath her broken wing,

and salty mucus dried under her eyes. The first bullet
shattered her keeled sternum, the second nestled

between her ribs, and the last darted through the middle
of the furculum, tearing away the pectoral's shield, rudely

entering the heart. That third bullet departed
out the back, framing a doorway in the mantle feathers

below the nape of her neck. She felt all of this
like the sudden emptiness after an egg descends,

the tired patience of waiting in a nest for days. She knew
the boys who did this, sensed their hidden sorrow.

The kind one who came first to these woods
after the bulldozers left, after so many trees had fallen

and been hauled away. It was he who sometimes fed her
bread. And the mean one she'd seen beaten by the father

and who now used his fists to forget. And the scared one
who stole his grandfather's .22, wanting to prove

he was tough to the kids who shoved and shouted
in line for the bus. Before she let go of the branch,

she squawked in her new voice, which was softer
and sounded like water splashing against rock.

The boys, who'd taken a stick to poke at her rigid corpse,
turned toward the tree where she perched

but could not see her because she'd changed. The one
who'd fed her said he was sorry they'd done this.

And the mean one hung his head and mumbled
that none of it meant shit. And the scared one

took the gun back home and put it in the basement
where so many secrets are kept.

For Jim Harrison

Aesthetics Precedes Ethics

The doors of the brook trout's pink gills open
and close as it wriggles in my palm, back
yellow and black, variegated like coral. Light appears
at the fish's exposed sides, and the sound of water
collects in backwash where the stream careens
over boulders, milk-white like the edging along the fish's
pelvic and anal fins. In hand, the caudal fin
flays orange and ebony, a nimbus of flame

haloing the body. The fish's eyes continue to hold
the caddis hatch, while the thread the stream holes
itself through makes a thin space between ridges.
I spread the net of my fingers in the water,
and the trout disappears beneath a ledge, as the stream
will, if I follow it high up into the mountain.

Signified

Under a Montana sky, blue-black with smoke from August fires,
the weight of my line unspools, pushing away from the fly rod

in cursive loops. Where the water calms, the cliffside shimmers
in the creek's mirror, looking back at itself while asking

what is artifice, what is real. That's how it feels to make a poem
out of the movement of water and fish: a cutthroat pierces the riffle,

rips the fly down into the current. I want language to curve
into a question, like the shape the rod takes as it allows the trout

to play out aggression, our fear of lost freedom. Line buzzes
as it's stripped from the reel, running over stone-rubble where

with each hard rain, or the torrent of snowmelt in spring, the course
of water is changed. When a trout leaps, unmoored by air, it can spit

the hook, unraveling meaning and remaking the time spent reading
the flow, determining which flies have hatched. Thankfully, one glides

into the net, as I search for the words to help remove the flattened barb
from memory's sharp-toothed jaw.

Fire Suppression

*We humans
are smaller than they, and crawl
unnoticed,*

about and about the smoky map.
—DENISE LEVERTOV

Every time the lightning struck the match
of a fir or spruce limb, we blew it out,
set backfires and dug trenches. With the forest
smudged in smoke, brittle, drier with each summer,
I struggled not to lose my way. Making the jump
was easy, floating above the visible world
in a haze. I navigated by the blue of three streams
that braid and collect in the sink of a modest lake.
Most of the fires we start are small.
You can barely hear them whisper.
Blue flame beneath a kettle. The flicker
of light from a candle. Even the log that snaps
and sparks in the hearth is conversational.
But when I heard the wildfire scream
along the canyon wall, unbearable heat
forming at its mouth, I understood
the meaning of profane. First seven mule deer
leapt past. Then a cow moose with two calves
galloped by. Four bear followed, as well as eight
bighorn sheep, several mink and pika, a herd
of elk, a skulk of fox, and too many coyote
to count. Colliding in the face of sure predation,
the fire owned three sides of the scorching net,
and like the sun, it wanted to burn itself into a circle.
I discarded my ax, my pack, the doubt that slowed
my feet. In pursuit, the heavy musk of exertion

and fear drowned my ragged breath, and the cadence
of hooves and claws tore through my voice, echoes
crossing the basin of water I'd seen from the sky:
the promise we'd all be immersed in its depths
as fire seared the air above our heads.

Whip-poor-will

Without bird song how would we know the sun is the cut skin
of an orange rolled into a circle and laid flat, last fading hour pinned
to a pine before any star allows itself to be seen? Or that night
is a gray fox stalking a ruffed grouse, coveting the heart
and plump breasts? There are too many ways of knowing
to account for, and most seem ill-suited to the way we live now.
In September boneset blossoms in the old hayfield, fragrant whitecaps
curling around us. Why should I keep this joy a secret, hidden
in the wheel ruts a tractor cut fifty years ago? In teaching me the names
for trees and birds, my father neglected to say that like an alluvial wash
broken bits of shell and sand can wear away words. In May I followed
a blood trail back to a coyote den dug under the twisted root ball
of a fallen maple. No one was home. Having smelled me
from a long ways off, the mother moved her pups; what was left
of a fawn's leg still showed her teeth marks. When the hurricane
took out most of the Jersey coast, the winds on its backside howled
for two days straight. Here on the Allegheny Front I found
the shredded lung of a hornet's nest beneath a chestnut oak, last
of the buzzing like the slow hiss of a punctured tire.
At thirty I began to write down all the names of the dead
so they wouldn't disappear. With the moon full up
on the tip of the ridge and the picking ladders still standing
in the orchard, nightjars feed on moths gone crazy
in the trembling light. A friend likes to call them bullbats,
but the trilling of their music betrays kindness
in the names they use for themselves.

II.

Salvelinus fontinalis

*By the time you hold the native in your hands it is you who
has been caught; you who shines, and feels like silver; you
who came, long ago, from water; you who suddenly can't
live without this beautiful river.*

—DAVID JAMES DUNCAN

The water's footsteps descend the stairs
of the mountain, digging pools
where native brook trout feed and lay down
their seed in redds, where even more water
forces its way up through the gravel
ushering in the young-of-the-year.

Springs rise everywhere in this stream,
struggling to forgive us the mines we tunneled
and left behind in a century we try to forget.
Partway up the mountain acid mine drainage
seeps from the punctured side of the ridge.
Iron sulfate sweeps down and banks
its orange flames in a grotesque tongue
of deceit. Scientists call it a "kill zone."
Nothing lives in its wake. We walk
more than a mile downstream
before we see the first crayfish
and further to find a lone brookie.

I spend most of my time searching
for these native fish. My wife asks
what I wish to do with them.
It's not about hunger, although
a few times each year I build
a small fire in a ring of stone, melt
butter in a cast iron skillet. How easily

the pink and white flesh departs
from needle-thin bones and fingers
bring quivering meat
to the tongue, sweet muscle
that lashed the body to the current
and now fixes itself to the threads
of my flesh.

I suppose another kind
of hunger causes me to cradle
them, to long for a connection
with that life hidden
in rock-seams, the breach
of boulders, white foam
of oxygen fashioned by water
falling over downed beeches
and hemlocks.

At fifty my eyes have begun to fail.
Before it all goes dark
I want to take in
the dimensions of each fish,
arrange their bodies on moss beds
and capture what I've missed
in a photograph. I'll return
to these pictures when sleep
offers no reverie as improbable
as the dream of creation
and the forever-shifting fantasy
of evolution that caused this Atlantic char
to convert, to become landlocked
in a creek most mapmakers ignore.

We all worship something.
I'll take the beauty and strength
of these fish, holy and godlike,
with backs vermiculated
so you can't see them as they fan
above strewn rocks at your feet.

I've caught myself praying to them,
hoping such prayers might help them
save themselves, and because I can't
escape the religion of my youth,
I still believe God is one, or at least three-
in-one, the world drenched by the Holy
Spirit of this fish's colors.

Stepping along the bank,
I crush wild mint with my boot.
The fragrance rises into the June air,
reminding me of the mint we grew
at the back steps of the farmhouse
and the friend who would drape
his fish in these pungent
leaves at the bottom
of his creel, keeping the fish
fresh for the evening meal.

Consider each cell trembling
in my hand as I hold
this fish that gives me faith;
or the scales that cover its side
and quake as it fights at the end

of my line; or the life that runs
through rushing water, and the gravity
that forces that water down
the slope of this mountain
in which these ever-moving bodies
bless us with their unceasing
faithfulness.

If you've been in a room
when someone dies
after a long illness,
then you know how
sight recedes, how
the dying fade from
the physical body, the silence
somehow different: not the lack
of sound but its absence.

In high school I read about
the transmigration of souls,
and later in college
about how the sun would go out
and the earth would cease to be.
I wonder where these souls will go
when that day comes.

Here the hermit thrush breaks
the stillness as it praises
the river and all those that reside
within its banks. I've seen the bird's notes
written in a field guide as *oh, holy holy,*

ah, purity purity, eeh, sweetly sweetly.
Who could argue with that?

I wish I could sing just a few of those lines,
but only a croak flies out of my mouth.
As vast as the green world seems
when I'm inside this seam of forest
that was nearly destroyed,
I know we've been left a fragment
of what ought to be here.

So many of us have the urge to travel
long distances, to escape the place
we were born or find ourselves
consigned to. I don't drive my pickup
more than ten miles in any direction.
The news of the universe I'm interested in
is written on the sides of these fish.

At the edge of the riffle's white curling
I count three brookies looking up
for a terrestrial to float by, a chance to dart
skyward, to sip the surface with open jaws.
As the fish grow older, longer in tooth,
I understand better what Wang Wei wrote
after the death of Yin Yao: *Of your bones,*
now buried white cloud, this much remains
forever: streams cascading empty
toward human realms.

III.

At the Raptor Rehabilitation Center

The crippled and the lame rise up with a clatter. Feathers
broken and disheveled. Nubs where wings should be. Even
empty sockets, which make it impossible to judge the distance
as a mouse or sparrow flees. The woman who feeds them,
who cares for their every need, wakes before the sun
and strokes the knife across a stone, hoping the chickens
she sacrifices will feel mercy in a sharpened blade.
In the dim light, her husband reads the paper, drinks
coffee as black as newsprint. He gathers the blood-
speckled heads near the stump, lends a hand to corral
aimless bodies running for help. Long before the school busses
arrive, or families in station wagons drive through the gate,
talons rip death's gift, and these birds sing riotous hymns
of praise for the sweet brutality in this woman's hands,
for the simple offering her loving kindness brings.

Carnivore

This is my body, which is given for you; do this in remembrance of me.

—LUKE 22:19

I slept, and in my sleeping
became the things I loved
and killed. More than twenty
deer. Nearly fifty cows.
Eighty-five hogs
and thirty-one lambs.
Countless rabbits
longing to mate in their dens,
and ninety-three squirrels
searching the treetops
for leafy nests. Sixty-six
of the best tasting ducks, teal
and ring-necked divers,
presented at the feet
by a good dog's jaws,
by a canine persistence
I'm still learning to obey.
I slaver at the sound of geese
flying over the tops of sycamore
in the flood plain. I'm a slave
to the memory of each one
I've plucked and gutted, the many
animals I've butchered and eaten,
so when I rise from the pool
of blood my dreams float in,
the fire sparks with dripping fat,
with the smell of my own
burning flesh consumed
in the body's oven.

Burn Barrel

A girl is throwing trash at the flames.
Anything that will burn. Plastic milk jugs,
cardboard boxes, the electric panels
of broken toys and the needled syringes
her mother uses to shoot insulin
into her thighs. The fire smolders, gray-
to-black-to-purple, mutating into a green
plume like the peacock feather she bought
when her class took a trip to the zoo.
She slips a caramel between her lips, stolen
from her grandmother's pink candy dish.
She watches snow fall and the wind blow
across the mouth of the barrel, whistling
smoke into a field of corn-stubble, shading
a trail to the edge of the woods where each day
it grows dark a little earlier. She hears
the snowplow on the county road, sees sparks
as the blade strikes asphalt. When her stick
stirs what's left of the flames, she feels
the sugar in her body rise against the barrel
that warms her. She feeds the fire
that melts the sky.

For Paula Bohince

Chorale for the Newly Dead

His back to an oak, the boy sat
in a ring, having cleared the dead
leaves so as not to make a noise.

Guns fired up the hollow, and he
imagined deer falling, a line
of lung-blood drawn down
behind them.

He was grateful
no animal came to him
and let the rifle lay
across his lap.

Someone ran dogs along the ridge.
Although it was illegal
it made pushing deer easier.

In summer, with corn and beans
in the fields, the crows stayed
in the valley. Now less warmth
brought beating wings
to mountainsides.

With so much killing,
gut-piles crowded the forest,
and the boy closed his eyes,
drifted with the slant of red
that reminded him
of a fox's coat in May.

For the rest of the day
he listened to the chorus
of dark birds
but refused to join
in their gossip.

October Gloriole

The soft light at day's end runs
through the backs of red tupelo
leaves, forming a nimbus,
and higher up, where limbs
and branches part, a wandering sky
rivers the dark with glinting stars
we cannot see.

Ornithological

A friend's son has a head of bird song, of bird calls
full of hunger and the primal joy that wells into a cry
at the back of the throat. If you wonder, no, this isn't
metaphor. Even his mother can tell you
where a green-throated warbler hides in the leaves,
or how the great crested flycatcher roosts in an oak.
What she knows she learned in a classroom while he
glided from her womb with lips pursed. A life list
is something that follows no matter where you perch,
and the number of birds that flock behind him
could block out the sun. He studies flyways, suffers
fall and spring migrations, scowls at his useless arms
in frustration. Once in September, hiking an abandoned
logging road in a narrow ravine, he held up his hand,
quieted us so we might hear the Kentucky warbler
passing overhead. All we heard was the sound
of the stream below, until he moved his fingers,
as if stitching a song in the air, tracing the beats
with each lilting note, wedding us to earth
as the bird winged south.

For Carl Engstrom

Fenestration, an Eclogue

In September purple asters shine around a yellow eye, intricate
as the bone webbing at the base of a rabbit's skull. At midday
fox sleeps in his burrow after a meal of mice, and crow

sits under an apple tree so the blackest parts of its body
may collect the dwindling heat. I pick windfalls to peel and pare,
half-moons placed side by side in a pan. The smallest bones

of the hand filter light as it falls through yellow birch leaves,
while along the ridge, high in the black gum tree, cedar waxwings
call to one another to eat more of the sapling's dark berries.

This time of year the dwindling brightness matters, multiplying
a skeleton of shadows. With bone so fine, speed comes easily.
See: just now in the garden the rabbit outruns the fox.

Winterkill

Because the day disrobes, discards scarf and sweater,
exposing April's white skin, I go singing
into the longer light, walking and fishing and gathering
the bright red teaberries that grow sweeter through the cold
months and now taste like fresh mint cut from a summer garden.
And in this I find the bones of animals who starved,
or were run down by coyotes or wild dogs leaping over
the deeper snow, who also felt hunger gnawing at their bones.
Here the rib of a yearling doe points through the canopy
of May apples, while near the stream the skull of a porcupine
sleeps in a deathbed of quills, softened by the petals
of the first yellow violets.

The Field Moving Inside the Field

Wind blows through night

      across a field of wheat. Wind stops

near dawn, and four deer who walked

      in dark beneath hemlocks along the river

step from the woods

      into the openness of grain.

The field becomes a daybed

      where deer rest as they mark

the sun's passage: solitary oak

      near the center of the field

like a sundial's pin. When they grow

      thirsty, deer remember the river,

willowy legs crushing stalks of wheat

      as they leave narrow trails

that show how energy disperses.

Visible Spectrum

We both believe and disbelieve a thousand times an Hour,
which keeps Believing nimble.
—EMILY DICKINSON

June light drapes itself
across the hay shocks
Jacob Peachey gathered
with his sons
yesterday afternoon.

New grass already sprouts
at the base, and in a few days,
when the hay dries, he and his sons
will lay up the shocks in the loft.

I don't think Jacob knows
how Monet painted haystacks
obsessively, stepdaughter
wheeling canvases in a barrow
so he might work at refining
the aspect of light
as it slid down the roof.

This time of year the sun
appears a little before five
and lasts until nearly ten.
Jacob values the light
that illuminates the work
he and his sons must do.

Next week he'll send
his milking cows
into the field
to eat what fell
and was left behind,
as well as what's new
and just growing.

I wonder what the grass feels
as the cows tongue
each blade, releasing the light
that's been stored
through April and May.

Jacob faithfully studies
the light, notes
with nimble believing
the way it ripples
over everything
it touches.

After mucking stalls,
some days, like Monet,
Jacob counts the layers
of light, marvels
at such fragility, his hand
passing through the visible
spectrum, as the sun
slips into the gaps
and climbs the barn's
rough boards.

After Considering My Retirement Account

The last week of May the chokecherry trees flower.
I tell my wife these are the finest hours to fish for brook trout.
Foam flower and Canada Mayflower cast their fragile blossoms
out of last year's losses, proving once again that death is the key
to fecundity. In the midst of all this fragrance the woods
become a leaf-house that's paid for. Yesterday my friend's brother
was convicted of embezzling their parents' estate. We should never steal
from those who come before us or borrow from those who come after.
Because there's a cost for what sparkles beneath the surface,
we eat the fish we catch right down to the bones.
I know we'll never be rich. This time of year Clintonia's
emerald leaves line the river's banks, and I work hard to calculate
the number of days before the round globe of their blooms
reach maturity.

Self Portrait with Fish and Water

In the world underwater, near the cattails where bass patrol
their spawning beds, early summer light clings to the turquoise sides
of pumpkinseed sunfish, so named because of the shape
their bodies take, not the coloration of their ctenoid scales, tangerine
stippling that stony blue, giving way to a yellow that seeps
to the base of the pelvic fin, an aquatic canvas as if painted
by the artist who cut away his own ear out of love, leaving
a blackened hole the sounds of his joyous screams rushed into,
a coal-dark flap like the one at the side of this fish's face,
which shows me the world is always receding, fleeing
the shape of my shadow as I walk these banks.

Final Complaint

In the last weeks when the drugs and the endless days of sitting
made it nearly impossible to shit, my father asked me to give him
an enema, makeshift, warm water mixed with salt in a red bucket,
as he'd taught me when I was thirteen at the animal clinic, the same
solution we used for dogs as sick as he was now, the oppression
of the tumor's growth crowding intestines. I offered to drive
to the drugstore, but he refused, frugal as his farmer-father, saying
this would do, telling me to draw the water into the plastic tube,
instructing me to insert its end between his withered flanks.
I squeezed through the groans, the mumbled *damn*s, the absurd
picture of a turkey baster crammed up my father's ass.
After three shots of this, he said *Enough!* and reached his hand
to loosen the stool, to pry it from its nesting like a fouled egg.
With ridiculous plops the dark pebbles fell into the toilet's
rusty water, tarnished coins at the bottom of a wishing well.

The Last Time My Mother Lay Down with My Father

How did he touch my mother's body
once he knew he was dying? Woods white
with Juneberry and the question of how
to kiss the perishing world, where to place
his arms and accept the gentle washing
of the flesh. With her breast in hand
did he forgive with some semblance
of joy the final bit of fragrance
in the passing hour, the overwhelming
sweetness of multiflora rose, and the press
of her skin against his?

The body's cartography is what we're given:
flesh sloughing into lines and folds, the contours
of its mapmaking. When at last he died,
summer's heat banking against the windows,
she'd been singing to him, her face near to his,
and because none of us wanted it to end,
we helped her climb into bed next to him
where she lifted his hand to her chest
and closed her eyes.

Morning along the Little J, before the Hurricane Makes Landfall

We die only once, and for such a long time!
—MOLIÈRE

In the clear October shallows, water laps over the long stalks
of the heron's legs as the bird hunts bluegills in the first dark
smudges of rain. I never noticed its sharp bill matches the color
of poplar leaves that float like lanterns to guide the departed
into paradise, nor that its breast disappears into the scaling bark
of a sycamore tree whose roots run down the bank
and under the bottom of the stream. Like an unopened book,
instinct's dispatch is lost at the foot of our distracted days.
This isn't the first we've fished this stretch together:
my line circled across the moving water; the bird's
slow steps bringing muddy clouds to the surface.
My wife wants me home by noon, and soon this heron
will search out the safety of a riverine thicket.
Once, after a night of listening to the house
lashed by wind and rain, I found an egret
bent awkwardly in death, puzzled into the limbs
of an ash that had washed into a bend in the river.
I don't know if it was already dead when the tree
snagged the long cane of its neck, distending
the hollowed bones to the point of breaking.
Even days later there was no prying the body loose
to lay it properly to rest. Most sacred books tell us
not to worry, that even the birds of the air
will be cared for. In the time that's left
the flash of a sunfish will suffice, as I prepare
for the strike of that great bird's bill,
the longed-for tug at the end of my line.

Brief Meditation at Nightfall

The last of the sun is breaking the trees
up high on the western ridges, and close
to the ground the burnished copper of dying
fern smells like freshly cut hay. Near the cattails
that stand like a fence, deer bend their long necks
to drink, and I find clumps of buck scat, dark
globes made from even smaller globes.
In the orchard halfway up the hill
an apple my dead father called *King David*
grows redder as the earliest moonlight
drifts down over our skin, reminding us
we will all be ghosts to someone.

Monongahela Nocturne

Here is the alchemy of the grunt, the music that turns one thing into
another, the black air that waits beyond the doors of the foundry, long
nights spent in the blinding wake of the furnace that burns without
ever going out, eternal flame of the boss's making, sour breath that
belches across the face of the man who drives home after work in the
last of the dark and slides the door to his shed sideways, wrestles the
salt block he bought at the hardware store into the grove of aspen
behind his house where deer come to lick the white square at the
cusp of this waning moon, to taste something of the ancient salty sea,
which fills the bellies of these delicate beasts with dreams of Atlantic
cod swimming in circles of loneliness, sullen fish hiding beneath an
island-shelf, frightened by the hunger of men, the knots of nets cast
from scarred and swollen hands, cheered by cruel mouths that speak
a language like the bark of harbor seals, all of them stunned by their
good fortune at not having to be changed, yet again, into something
else.

Ash Wednesday

Around eleven I hike the ridge in what's left

      of last night's wet snow. Overhead golden

eagles are passing up the flyway, while down the hollow

      the sound of water seeks the valley floor. Rain will start

from the west tonight, but for now the glossy leaves

      of mountain laurel shimmer. Every quarter hour

brings another of these great birds. Climbing

      the sharp crease in the ravine, I saw the first

bear tracks of the year, which help me to believe

      the dead will rise from the grave.

Wood Tick

Most of January two red-tailed hawks hunted the backyard, lifting
from a tamarack to float over the roof, circling back if a rabbit

or field mouse eluded talons, which opened and closed
with hunger's petition. When a neighbor's cat went missing

we kept ours inside, afraid we'd witness her orange and white legs
bicycling the air. On the mountain in Virginia where we put

what little remained of my father, the man digging the grave told me
that once, right as the minister said the beloved lived in eternity's kingdom,

a bear as big as a horse galloped between headstones,
eight dogs howling at its heels, until it fell into an open grave

and broke its hind legs. Here in the ridge and valley of Pennsylvania,
the bones of a ten-year-old girl who'd gone missing were found

riddled with the teeth marks of coyotes. We never recovered
her clothes or schoolbag, and after she was laid in the ground

her family moved away. Near mid-December in the hemlocks
above our house I came across a circle of feathers—no bones,

not even the red edge of spilled blood. A white line of scat
showed the bird's surprise; a bobcat's tracks explained

the advantage of a suitable perch. When I hunt
I sit twenty feet in the air, back against a maple, bottom

on the ladder-seat's steel grill. In the morning, as the stars
vanish, cedar waxwings descend to the branches around my head

and eat the tree's small seeds. After days in the woods,
sometimes I'll find a tick along my hairline, belly distended,

bloated on the blood none of us wish to spare.
Leo Beech worked for my father at the animal hospital

and lived in a trailer out near the swamp. He mowed
and kept the kennels, showed me how to take the end

of a cigarette and push it into the back of a tick.
Most of the time it wriggled out from under the skin,

shrugged off its mortal appetite. But if the damned thing
wouldn't let go, Leo bent and breathed in, burning ember

of tobacco glowing: oxygen's star turned to ash as I watched
the tick's head blaze, buried dead beneath the flesh.

How Our Children Know They'll Go to Heaven

Before she's even thought of the sun, she's awake
in the last of the dark, tearing old sheets into strips,

soaking them in a tin pail of kerosene. Her mother
binds her wrists and waist to ward off chiggers.

In the blackberry patch the bugs feast on the most
delicate flesh, and to help her forget she pretends

each berry is a jewel, slowly rounding the dimpled
blackness, the crevices that hide the seed's sharp tines.

In church she's told she must suffer to enter paradise,
and so she gives thanks for the bittersweet

juice that runs from the corners of her mouth, sour
nectar staining teeth and tongue, dirtying the whorls

of her fingertips. When she gets home her nails
are bloody from scratching bites, and she leaves

red and black prints her mother finds on the frame
of the pantry door, marking her as one of the saved.

Circus Train Derailment

McCann's Crossing, Tyrone, Pennsylvania, 1893

At the bottom of the mountain
in the early morning light
the wrecked wheel
of a passenger car
turns in the air,
while across a fallow field
the sound of a water pump's
windmill keeps time.

Forty-nine horses lie
crushed beneath an overturned
stock car, legs painted red
like the wooden spindles
on a merry-go-round.

The animals who survive
listen to the emptiness
of stunned absence
and soon discover
that only their will
cages them.

The elephant shrugs,
shoulders breaking
through shattered boards
and bent nails.

A tiger slides through twisted
bars and bounds away
across a section of wheat
to eat a milking cow.

Among honeysuckle bushes
clouding the banks of a stream,
the snake charmer, whose head
bleeds through a turban, searches
for his anaconda, even as a possum
loses its way in the tunnel
of the snake's throat.

Camels peer into the distance
at a barn that rises like a pyramid
and with their oddly elongated strides
lope through new corn, passing
a section of fence where a bull's
sphinxlike head portends
a dire prophecy.

Wild grapevines drape the limbs
of oak and tulip poplar, and the organ
grinder's monkey swings to the top
of the canopy to sit in the crown
of a tree and contemplate
the geometry of a half-finished
clear-cut.

The townspeople bring wagons
to help remove the debris from the rails,
providing what salve they can as they try
to salvage the clowns' shoes and recover
the swords the girl with the long ponytail
swallowed at center ring.

The bear, who pulled a cart
in which small children rode
for a penny, slinks up the mountain,
finding two others who look like himself.
Together they sprawl
beneath the insubstantial fragrance
of white blossoms that will ripen
into the blackest of black
blackberries.

IV.

Turning the Compost at 50

The ants have returned and even the simplicity of lust fails me.
Watermelon, muskmelon, the slippery foam of cantaloupe. The wind
keeps blowing out of the south where rain gathers to plan its trip north.
In June, along the forest road where I pick raspberries, I find used condoms,
red, blue, flesh-colored, trying futilely to love the earth. Urine
restores nitrogen to dirt. What does the spent jism of teenagers replace?
Last November, high on the ridge, I spread my father's ashes in a wild
blueberry field for the bonemeal upon which my grief might grow plump
and ripe. When I dump melon rinds on the compost, hundreds of ants
scatter, then scramble back onto the pile, their mandibles clacking
in a raucous song of appetite.

Ode Scribbled on the Back of a Hunting Tag

She came down at an angle off the ridge, graceful
and curved like the last of the moon. Now she slumps
in the snow: cage of her torso emptied. The naked woods
hide little. A branch has been broken, forced sideways
to open her chest and cool the meat. In the end she offered
a half-sprinted stumble. But who doesn't look awkward in death?
Her hooves point uselessly in the wrong direction, neck
bent by the weight of the head, and her tongue dangles
from her mouth in defiance of what I did.

How Animals Forgive Us

*The greatest peril of life lies in the fact that human food
consists entirely of souls.*
—AUA, INUIT SHAMAN

Too many of our apples end up overripe, rotting
on the ground where skunks scavenge them
until they're drunk on fermented sugar
and stagger away into the speeding darkness
of the county road.

The farmer's dog brings groundhogs to his backdoor,
half-dead and squirming at the gates of what surely
must come next. According to Novalis, nothing
is ever complete, which makes this more bearable
and saves the farmer from having to gas them
in their dens.

Fishing the Ausable, I spied an otter on the far bank
and recalled that Sir Izaak Walton encouraged the killing
of waterborne weasels, simply because they ate the trout
he wished to catch. Moving upstream, the otter slid
into the luxury of water, its body's parenthesis arcing,
then vanishing in one grace-filled motion, leaving
an empty space for the eddy's current.

In the mountains above our house more than
twenty bear die each year. I refuse to hunt them
because when they rise up on hind legs
I see my dead father walking toward me,
and who wants to taste the meat that ushers in
such bitter dreams?

69

Over the river, trico flies hatch and merge
in mating swarms, delicately smudging the air
with their sex. On such days I've seen brown trout
float by, looking like men in business suits practicing
to drown: heads just above waterline, eyes glazed
with lust for the prize of sustenance.

This afternoon, a westerly wind wrinkles
the grassy waves in the field where, as a boy,
I buried dogs who died in my father's care.
Here I learned that the dead hearts of animals
wait for rain to repeat their lost rhythms,
although nothing, it seems, can resurrect them.

The northern shrike is named "butcher bird,"
because it skewers what it kills, then eats
its fill. I've found voles and field mice,
even the weightless bodies of songbirds, pierced
and saved on the hawthorn's long spikes,
a cache of drying flesh curing in the sun,
which makes good sense during lean winters.

Tonight at the supper table my mouth is filled
with meat, as I gnaw the bones of the deer
I watched eat pears from the neighbor's tree.
Some of the fruit still bends the branches, planets
suspended in space: chartreuse skins
tendering a grainy flesh, slicked with the taste
of honey, and what I imagine is the soul's
satisfying sweetness.

Reading Entrails

The Babylonians believed in prophecy hidden
beneath skin, hepatoscopy, interested in the liver,
the seat of life and the dark river of blood
that might offer a message from God.
Every Thursday my parents fried liver
and onions in cornmeal and butter.
It all tasted bitter, like the coffee that stained
my grandmother's teeth. Even when her dentures
slipped and slurred her speech, she spoke
as if she saw the future on an oracular TV.
Yesterday afternoon, arms elbow-deep
in a deer's chest cavity, I told my son the names
for the viscera: organs turkey vultures and ravens
pick at as offal. What might be divined
from this marbled flesh? The girl he will meet
and marry? A child he will love with worry?
A father he will carry to the grave?

Translation Problems

People search for cloud roads
but cloud roads can't be found
—HAN SHAN

All kinds of distances separate us.

A death more than a thousand years old.

The oceans that roll between continents, covering a bridge that once connected our lands.

When others sought you, you laughed and became part of the mountain.

It's written that Nicodemus and Joseph of Arimathea took Jesus's dead body to prepare it with spices and oils.

Did vultures and ravens do the same for you?

A bird's song can be discerned by the tracks it leaves in the snow.

What did the sky and the stars sing for your burial?

I keep hoping in death the mountain will swallow me, translating my body into some new language.

What's the word, I wonder, for the last poem anyone will ever write?

Epistemology, with July Moon

To forget the self is to awaken into the ten thousand things.
—DOGEN ZENJI

I'm convinced old maps are prayers.
When the self is forgotten, like a bird
along a stream, the yellowed paper unfurls
to disclose lines huddled together, suggesting
how steep the climb will be. Ascending
the southern ridge that cups its breath
around the lives of other animals,
my friend uses GPS, checks the instrument
again and again. Despite the claims
for precision, someone has to do ground-truthing,
a confirmation of the satellite's gaze.
This ravine—where shadows of ravens fall
and their almost-human voices echo higher—
is frilled with laurel's pink flowers.
I'm not sure what's necessary
to unveil the world behind the world
we see. Botany is useful but can't tell us
what the first humans called the berries
we ate in the clearing. The hand
that drew the earth's outline on this map—
work stored in plats, alluding to the idea
of ownership—now rests in some grave.
How I wish I could shake it, show
its long-dead proprietor where I stand,
how this place, circumscribed by lines
and degrees, forever shifts, trembling
with the vibrations of atoms and tectonics.
In the valley the moon shines upon the stream
I've crossed for a third time, joining itself
to a river that flows east.

Poem Made of Sadness and Water

When the rescue divers found the boys
drowned in the river hole, twelve
feet deep and held under
by curved stone, which blocked
the sun so they could not tell
the direction their breath rose,
each had wrapped his arms
around his friend, the one
who dared the other to swim,
and the other, who, seeing
his friend row the air, then
vanish, leapt in, only to lose
his way in the current
that hid this strange place

from their parents
and where they spied
the yellow and red iridescence
trout store at their sides
and the muskrat's webbed
feet clawing the hole
in the bank's mud wall
and a willow log
with bits of black leaf
swirling around the dead
branches, which reminded them
of the tadpoles they caught
and kept in jelly jars.

The Light around the Little Green Heron

Cattail, pickerel
weed, the umber
at ridgeline
that envelops
the sun. More hoop
than halo, holy
glowing, like coals
before they cool.
You'd think
these bluegills
that swim
at the bird's feet
could see
such illumination,
which brings with it
the beautiful threat
of death
from on high.

Monarchs

The children search milkweed
for yellow and black caterpillars.
They find two in the entire field,
confirming the reports
of precipitous decline.
The boy asks
if they might be changed
into something new, able
to fly on wings toward safety.
Anything's possible,
but we must consider history.
We've cut the ridges three times,
and where the earth was flat
stripped it for coal.

At the local museum
the curator entertains tourists
with stories of small boys
who fell through pit kiln roofs,
burned by charcoal fires
used to forge iron for cities
and ships that sailed the future.
More will disappear. Our passenger
pigeon, a footnote
tied to a taxidermied leg.
When I was a boy,
rivers caught fire
and all the fish died
in Lake Erie. Now some swim
without tumors.
When I spy a stray monarch
lighting on the head

of butterfly weed,
its stained-glass hinges
remind me
that the doors of a church
should stay open.

Canticle for Native Brook Trout

Now we are all sitting here strangely
On top of the sunlight.
—JAMES WRIGHT

Fishing the narrow stream
of light, we follow a seam
between hemlock and sweating
rhododendron, tulip poplar
and white oak that grow
more than a hundred feet tall.
The small fish that have been here
for thousands of years
lay in on flat rock that lines
the streambed, or hide beneath
the shelves where water
pours over fallen trees.
They are nearly invisible,
backs colored like the stone
in the pool where they were born
and where they will die
after giving birth to their own.
The drift of our flies
tempts them, and through
the glass surface we see
their jaws part, predatory
surge ending with a struggle
to be freed from the end
of our lines. Their lives
depend upon the coldness
of water, upon our desire
to touch their bodies,
to marvel at the skin
along their spines: the tan

worm-shaped ovals,
the smallest red circles,
the splash of yellow
and orange that washes
around their bellies
as we release them
and they swim
from our grasp
back into a sliver
of sunlight.

Silkworm Parable

We desire the mulberry leaf. Simple
industry of hunger. Spinning a thread
around ourselves while trying to make
something lovely of what's left.
The tree's fruit is too sweet, and silk's
beauty remains fragile. When we gaze up
at the blackness, the stars vanish
into the light we've cast toward heaven.

For Dan Gerber

July Letter to Chris D.

Today I walked in a couple of miles on a stream named after a guy
who's been dead more than 200 years. Hard not to stop at every wide
place in the run, but I limited myself to the ones where native brook
trout and the sun's current collide, a thing you once called bonelight
while trying to describe a canyon you were fishing, which made
me think about the intricate skeletons of these fish and the fallen
trees that change the flow of water and this skull I'm looking out of.
Rhododendron flowers weigh down their branches this time of year,
and with a spring rising every hundred feet, the streambed's cold seam
makes the hemlocks grow as tall as any building in our village. The
heat came up hard two days ago, air thick with water. Even the osprey
that hunt the reservoir halfway up the mountain stay put until the first
hint of darkness goads them from their perches and out over the lake
where the fish aren't quick enough to escape plummeting shadows.
To the south, coal cars line up by the thousands, until they disappear
under the trestles immigrants built during the first part of the last
century. When the air clears in October, you can see from Altoona to
Tipton, ten miles of valley floor lined with old ladders and what we
dig from deep under our feet. Most of August the heat bears down the
dust, so you'd be lucky to see halfway to my house. I haven't stopped
sweating since Sunday, not even to sleep, and sumac and nettles
balloon absurdly. On the back end of the Mill's farm, I saw a tree roped
with a poison ivy vine as thick as a python, and berry knots that looked
like mutated grapes. Where I parked the truck near the trailhead, tiger
swallowtails clustered on top of each other in a great fluttering, pulsing
heap of yellow, black, and indigo. I knelt to take some pictures and
improvised the sign of the holy church of migration, offered thanks
that we haven't wrecked the world completely. I'd hate to live in a place
that didn't have room for the beauty of these silken pollinators or the
rough husk of a hornet's nest. Come September I'll spend Saturday
afternoons watching honeybees and yellow jackets rock the long stems
of goldenrod, their black and yellow bodies moving back and forth in a

lovely sexual vibrancy. Heading deep into the forest, it's harder for dark thoughts to control me. Right now I'm listening to the water moving over the rocks, pushing my hand down through its fluid surface, breaking the plane and watching the refraction of light illuminate my disembodied fingers as they slant into what appears to be another dimension. I like to think about the intelligence of water, how it can read gravity's map, finding the quickest path to the valley floor. In here you never have to be lost. Game trails lead you to the best pools, like this one that measures fifteen by fifteen at the mouth and spoons to less than half that. It's more than deep enough to cover me, and the trout are hospitable, making room for my anxiety as I try to figure what to do with this world we'll leave too soon. For today, at least, I don't plan on heading down mountain until well past dark. In the meantime I'm going to strip to what I was born in, spend the rest of the day feeling my body go numb, the kind of relief I'd hoped would set in.

Revelation

You can wait for months, even years,
before seeing a bobcat or bear.
Moose scat isn't hard to find
if you know the right place to look.
But try locating the moose itself.
The queen bee hides in the deepest
chamber: worker bees the only evidence
she resides there. Revelation is like that.
Depending on the genus of myth,
there's less than one per square mile.
They need space to breathe, to forage.
Water to bathe and drink. Stories
to help piece together belief.
You'll have to take it on faith.
No one can walk quietly enough
to stalk them. If you're surrounded
by frail wings, don't think for a second
you had anything to do with it.
Your best shot is to stay put. In that half-light,
numinous at dawn and dusk, the thing
you've craved, and spent the better part
of your life searching for,
will pad noiselessly under
your tree-stand. Fur blacker
than a moonless night; musk
drifting with the smell of early spring.
You better hope it doesn't catch your scent,
or look up when you shift restlessly
in your seat. Remember if it approaches,
don't look directly into its face.
Instead bow your head
and cover your eyes.

Priest

My son says he sees God
in the face of every
fish he catches.
As he draws the deity nearer
to shore, he kneels
to cradle the fish
and lift it into the net,
to peer into the cosmos
in quivering bone
and colored scales.

If God is big enough,
and my son's hunger great,
he takes the priest,
carved from the hardest wood,
balances the cudgel in hand,
and strikes the fish
with as much mercy
as the act allows.

Benediction

When I pulled myself halfway up the rock face, arms
extended, legs ready to swing onto the shelf, I noticed

the timber rattler less than a foot from my face. He curled
around himself, like hands folded, like arms

thrown around the back of a friend. Recumbent and at rest,
for whatever reason he saw me as no threat, did not shake

his rattle, nor lengthen himself to slide like water
back beneath the earth. Instead he looked straight ahead,

satisfied with the shape his body had taken, with the heat
of the late spring sun, with the prayer he must have heard

me pray as I slid slowly back down the face of the rock,
my own body taking the shape of thanks.

Thieves

We filch
happiness
from the seed
pods of touch-
me-nots,
the explosion
of their husks
as they curl
backward
to expose
the future,
the leap
forward
into dreaming
dust, into
waiting out
winter
with hopes
a speckled
horn
will blossom
and bees
will crawl
inside it
to blow
a coupled
music.

Transfiguration of the Beekeeper's Daughter

Because the bees flew toward light the color of honey,
she couldn't see them but heard their hum, deep thrum
of the colony come out of the hive, comb dripping
with loss and the smoke her father used to subdue,
to pacify the fear that might spur an attack.

It wasn't until her brother began to cry that she noticed
her hair was moving, undulating like water easing
from a rapids, alive with an energy she recognized
as the gentle buzzing of hundreds and hundreds of bees.
They swelled along the strands of her hair, remaking

the small world that floated in front of her eyes,
as even more bees curled around her face.
She'd seen the woman at the fair who made a beard
of bees for the crowd of farmers and their families.
She read about the love and patience the woman told

the newsman was necessary as their legs and translucent
wings crept and fluttered across the tender flesh
under her chin, fanning cheekbones, slipping over
the helix of the outer ear. Like earrings cut
into the loveliest shapes, with colors of burnished

gold and copper, the bees poured over the girl's scalp,
some finding their way down the collarbone, onto arms
and breasts, abdomens pulsing in time to the electricity
along the hind legs that captured the pollen for the journey
back to the hive. She found it impossible to hold still

unless she thought of that bearded-bee woman,
the affection that transfixes the body
while even more bees conceal the feet and shins,
the knees and thighs, until a girl vanishes,
and in her place a winged seraph flies.

April Landscape, with Petals/Furrows/Wife

Willow blossoms deep in the lane, a rooster calls out at noon.
Young mulberry leaves are still sharp and less than green.
—FAN CH'ENG-TA

In the waning dark old apple trees set the ridgeside ablaze
with blossoms and bees, night's tenderness captured
in the vanishing ghost of a moon that peers down from Brush Mountain.
The other side of its face, which our youngest boy tells us is the sun,
shimmers in the forsythia we planted along the river before your father died.
With the trees as yet unleafed, spring light strikes with both love
and ferocity: no cover to be found as you place your skirt on the ground
between us. Despite the sky's sharp glance, nothing can keep us
from this buzzing. The world grows around itself with the wind's
threshed flowers, with bones and fieldstones pushed up from black soil.
This afternoon we've left the damp earth to dry in furrows, so tired
both of us sleep beneath the falling petals of a serviceberry tree.
In my arms you dream fitfully of fiddleheads unfurling, and I
of the boiling pot we'll cook them in.

89

August Hatch: Thinking of My Son after the Goldenrod Blooms

Brown trout swim in the deeper pools, seeking
cooler water farther down. The long yellow
flowers that conquered the field undulate
in the breeze that floods the banks.

Sun weakens, wind dies, and freshly hatched
caddisflies fill the air like dandelion seed
skirting riffles, shuttled along the surface
by the river's motion and their own brief flight.

More than a thousand years ago Po Chü-i
wrote in a poem: *We share all these
disappointments of failing autumn
a thousand miles apart.*

What I Know about Death and Resurrection

The dead fawn, bloated in the roadside heat the last two days,

      is alive again. Her side twitches as maggots writhe

the rib-cave, commas trying to connect the brief distance

      between life and death. The Gospels leave out the fact

that when Christ called forth the man who'd been dead

      for four days, those who loved him rushed forward

to wash the stink from his flesh. Soon there will be nothing

      left, except the leather of the deer's casing, the polished

sticks of its bones, tent poles to prop up faith

      when this second life departs.

          For K. A. Hays

Dreams of the Dead Father

Nearly four years after
I spread your ashes
around huckleberry bushes
on a talus slope that rises
over the forest where I hunt
and gather berries and fish
small streams for brook trout,
you still visit me.

Many days I look forward
to the darkness of sleep
that brings you back to life,
healthy, yet each of us knowing
the tumor will grow.

In this merciful limbo, together
we ski above tree line or snowshoe
the path to the hemlock grove
where we find the melted beds
made by sleeping deer.

In some dreams you take on
a different malady—a stroke
that jellies the right side
of your face, reducing speech
to a series of grunts, or a car accident
that leaves you without a hand
or leg, helpless to rototill
the garden or hay the meadow.

Sometimes you disappear
while my back is turned,
arm raised to point at a porcupine
teething a ring of bark
in the branches of an oak.

Usually you leave
with a simple goodbye.
Still able to walk
and cut the firewood
you'll need in December.

Acknowledgments

My thanks to the editors of the following journals or publications in which these poems first appeared, sometimes in different form.

American Literary Review: "Cenotaph"

Appalachia: "Monarchs," "What I Know about Death and Resurrection," and "Winterkill"

Arts & Letters: "Burn Barrel" and "By the Rivers of Babylon"

Blueline: "Ash Wednesday," "Ode Scribbled on the Back of a Hunting Tag," and "Wu"

Chautauqua: "The Last Time My Mother Lay Down with My Father"

Cheat River Review: "Mud Dauber" and "Yu"

Cumberland River Review: "Ornithological" and "Visible Spectrum"

The Fourth River: "Monongahela Nocturne"

Front Range Review: "After Considering My Retirement Account," "Circus Derailment," and "Epistemology, with July Moon"

Gray's Sporting Journal: "July Letter to Chris D." and "Sulphur Hatch"

Green Mountains Review: "April Landscape, with Petals/Furrows/Wife"

Hayden's Ferry Review: "What My Neighbor Tells Me Isn't Global Warming"

Image: "Homily" and "In a Dream William Stafford Visits Me"

Lake Effect: "How Our Children Know They'll Go to Heaven" and "Silkworm Parable"

The Missouri Review: "Fire Suppression"

New Madrid: "How Animals Forgive Us" and "Morning along the Little J, before the Hurricane Makes Landfall"

Notre Dame Review: "At the Raptor Rehabilitation Center" and "Drouth"

Orion: "Thieves" and "Turning the Compost at 50"

Poet Lore: "Poem Made of Sadness and Water"

Poetry East: "Afterlife"

Rattle: "Transfiguration of the Beekeeper's Daughter"
Sou'wester: "After the Third Concussion"
Spillway: "Brief Meditation at Nightfall"
Talking River: "Chorale for the Newly Dead" and "Wood Tick"
Tar River Poetry: "Signified"
Terrain.org: "Canticle for Native Brook Trout," "Grievous," and "Self Portrait with Fish and Water"
Watershed: "Benediction" (as "Late Spring Sun")
Water~Stone Review: "Translation Problems"
West Branch: "Fenestration, an Eclogue" and "Reading Entrails"

"In a Dream William Stafford Visits Me" was reprinted in *A Ritual to Read Together: Poems in Conversation with William Stafford*, edited by Becca J.R. Lachman and published by Woodley Press.

"The Last Time My Mother Lay Down with My Father" won the Editors Prize from *Chautauqua* and was nominated for a Pushcart Prize.

"Ornithological" was nominated for *Best of the Net* by *Cumberland River Review*.

All translations of the quoted lines from the poetry of Fan Ch'eng-ta, Han Shan, Po Chü-i, Tu Fu, and Wang Wei are by David Hinton.

Thanks to the following people for their continued encouragement as I make my poems throughout the days of the year: Lori Bechtel-Wherry, Wendell Berry, Brian Black, Paula Bohince, Marcia and Bruce Bonta, Dave Bonta, David Budbill, Cameron Conaway, Jim Daniels, Joyce Davis, Nathan Davis, Noah Davis, Shelly Davis, Chris Dombrowski, Tom Montgomery Fate, Don Flenar, Don and Punky Fox, Dan Gerber, Jane Hirshfield, Don and Melinda Lanham, Virginia Kasamis, Helen Kiklevich, Julie Loehr, Carolyn Mahan, Dinty Moore, Erin Murphy,

Sean Prentiss, Mary Rose O'Reilley, Steve Sherrill, Julie Reaume, Jack Ridl, Michael Simms, Annette Tanner, Jack Troy, Ken Womack, and Robert Wrigley.

And a special thanks to four wonderful poets and dear friends who read this book in various stages and helped to make it better: K. A. Hays, Mary Linton, Lee Peterson, and David Shumate.

I would also like to thank the H. J. Andrews Experimental Forest in Oregon for a writer's residency.

Finally, many of these poems were finished with the help of generous research grants from Pennsylvania State University.

Todd Davis is the author of five full-length collections of poetry—*Winterkill, In the Kingdom of the Ditch, The Least of These, Some Heaven*, and *Ripe*—as well as of a limited edition chapbook, *Household of Water, Moon, and Snow: The Thoreau Poems*. He edited the nonfiction collection, *Fast Break to Line Break: Poets on the Art of Basketball*, and co-edited the anthology *Making Poems*. His writing has been featured on the radio by Garrison Keillor on *The Writer's Almanac* and by Ted Kooser in his syndicated newspaper column *American Life in Poetry*. His poems have won the Gwendolyn Brooks Poetry Prize, the Chautauqua Editors Prize, the *Foreword Reviews* Book of the Year Bronze Award, and have been nominated several times for the Pushcart Prize. His poetry has been published in such noted journals and magazines as *American Poetry Review, Iowa Review, North American Review, Missouri Review, Gettysburg Review, Orion, West Branch*, and *Poetry Daily*. He is a fellow in the Black Earth Institute and teaches environmental studies, creative writing, and American literature at Pennsylvania State University's Altoona College.